What is corporate flight?

Corporate flight is the disinvestment of a corporation's capital—the running-down or liquidation of its net productive capacity—and its movement to other uses or locations, frequently outside of the United States.

Why is corporate flight a problem?

The problem is the real loss of jobs and income for millions of working people, and the social and economic devastation caused in families and communities which this often unanticipated corporate movement creates.

Are plant closings and movements primarily a regional problem?

There has been, for good reason, well-publicized commentary about plant closings in the Northeast and North Central regions—sometimes called the Frostbelt—and the older Eastern and Western states. Certainly this has produced considerable hardship in many older industrialized urban areas. But there is evidence that plant closings are occurring regularly in the Sunbelt as well, and that thousands of jobs are being lost to movement of corporate branches overseas, in search of cheaper labor.

Are our national economic problems responsible for these closings and capital movement?

Plant closings are not a recent phenomenon. The tremendous concentration of economic power in the hands of multinational corporations and conglomerates, and their ability to move their resources quickly and on a vast scale, have been building for decades. Corporate flight seems to proceed and grow—through good times and bad.

CORPORATE FLIGHT

THE CAUSES AND CONSEQUENCES OF ECONOMIC DISLOCATION

by
Barry Bluestone,
Bennett Harrison, and
Lawrence Baker

A Progressive Alliance Book
Washington, D.C.

Corporate Flight: The Causes and Consequences of Economic Dislocation
by Barry Bluestone, Bennett Harrison, and Lawrence Baker

Copyright © Barry Bluestone, Bennett Harrison, and Lawrence Baker
All rights reserved.
March 1981

Editorial Consultants: Deborah Davis, Nora Lapin

A Progressive Alliance Book
The Progressive Alliance/1757 N Street, N.W./Washington, D.C. 20036/
(202) 828-8530

Published with
The National Center for Policy Alternatives/2000 Florida Avenue, N.W./
Washington, D.C. 20009/(202) 387-6030
and
Working Papers for a New Society/186 Hampshire Street/Cambridge,
Massachusetts 02139/(617) 547-4474

ISBN Number: 0-89788-027-7

Photo credits:
Pages 10-11, 77: David Welsh
Pages 17, 31, 47, 53, 58-59, 62, 67, 87: Russ Marshall
Pages 22, 41, 73: Earl Dotter
Pages 78-79: Morelli (OPIC)
Page 83: Nicholl (OPIC)
Page 91: Henry Babson
Page 95: Cliff Kalick

Printed by union printers

THE AUTHORS

BARRY BLUESTONE is Associate Professor of Economics and Director of the Social Welfare Research Institute at Boston College. He is at work on a major project which is modeling the distributional consequences of federal tax transfer and expenditures policy. He lives in Newton, Massachusetts.

BENNETT HARRISON is Associate Professor of Economics and Urban Studies at the Massachusetts Institute of Technology, and is the author of the forthcoming book *The Transformation of the New England Economy since World War II* (MIT-Harvard Joint Center for Urban Studies, Summer 1981). He lives in Brookline, Massachusetts.

LAWRENCE BAKER is Co-Publisher of the magazine *Working Papers,* and is a Fellow of the National Center for Policy Alternatives in Washington, D.C. He is at work on a book project studying cost/benefit analysis and regulatory economics. He lives in Cambridge, Massachusetts.

FOREWORD AND ACKNOWLEDGEMENTS

As many of those who are involved with the problem of economic dislocation will recognize, this book is in many ways a direct descendant of an earlier work by my co-authors entitled *Capital and Communities*. Published by the Progressive Alliance in 1980, this groundbreaking study is now, unfortunately, out of print.

Messrs. Bluestone and Harrison are currently revising and updating their original work for another book, *Capital and Communities: The Causes and Consequences of Private Disinvestment in American Industry,* to be published in 1982 by Basic Books. It will include as part of its new material a thorough examination of the relationship between economic dislocation and the so-called "reindustrialization" of America.

Dozens of people played some role in the publication of the original *Capital and Communities,* and the recognition of their contributions ran almost two full pages. This book owes a debt to each, but there are a special few who played such a major part in this undertaking that they should be given acknowledgement here. First on that list should be the person who is most responsible for the publication of both books: Bill Dodds, Executive Director of the Progressive Alliance. Without his commitment to solving the problems of plant closings and economic dislocation, and his sturdy faith in the capacities of the trade union movement, together with his continuing support of those people writing and working on these issues, this book would simply not exist.

Our particular thanks also go to Edgar James, the former Associate Director of the Progressive Alliance whose energies carried this project through its first several months; Nora Lapin, who edited *Capital and Communities* and also participated in the conception of this book; Deborah Davis, who provided valuable editing help at several stages; Barbara Griffith, Virginia Richardson, Carol Ridner, Sheila Knodle and especially Carol Fitzgerald, all of whom helped in the production or editing of the manuscript; and Andrew Bornstein, who designed and produced the book itself.

Special note should be made of the staff of *Working Papers* magazine, particularly Bob Kuttner and Charles Knight, whose interest in this subject produced a useful article based on an important part of *Capital and Communities,* and who have supported the idea of this book for close to a year.

We hope this is a book for activists. As such, it is dedicated to those people both within the labor movement and without who will continue the fight against unrestrained corporate flight in the years ahead.

Lawrence Baker
Cambridge, Massachusetts
March, 1981

CONTENTS

Chapter One
THE PROBLEM

HEADLINES TELL the story, with ominous frequency: Plant Closing, Thousands to Lose Jobs. Company Blames Rising Costs, Moves Operations Overseas. State Offers Tax Abatements to Keep Industry from Moving South. Area Economy Depressed by Layoffs.

New England, New Jersey, California, Ohio, Alabama, Kansas; electronics, tires, textiles, automobiles, chemicals. No matter what area of the country or industry is examined, chances are that during the last several years many plants have been abruptly moved or shut down and that thousands of workers have been displaced or thrown out of work.

This is the story of corporate flight—the movement by business of capital and resources within the United States, or out of the country altogether, leaving economic and social wreckage in its wake. It is a story which for millions of Americans has become a tragedy. For example:

The New York Times (November 28, 1979)
"The United States Steel Corporation announced yesterday that it was closing 15 plants and mills in eight states. About 13,000 production and white-collar workers will lose their jobs. The cutback represents about 8 percent of the company's work force. The retrenchment was one of the most sweeping in the industry's history . . . in spite of high demand for steel in the last two years."

The Wall Street Journal (August 7, 1978)
"Southern Airways, Inc. said it plans to fire 14 percent of its workforce so it can afford $65 million of airplanes. The air carrier said it is firing 500 employees over the next two weeks in a move that will save Southern an estimated $7.5 million over the next 12 months. 'One of the quickest ways to reduce expenses,' said Mr. Taylor (director of public relations), 'is to reduce people.' "

Cleveland Plain Dealer (January 11, 1978)
"After 77 years, Goodyear Tire and Rubber Company is ending production of conventional automobile tires in Akron, Ohio. The phase-

out will result in the loss of about 730 production and salaried jobs . . . A new $180 million radial tire production plant at Lawton, Oklahoma will begin operations early next year . . . (and) within the next few months it will begin production at a $69 million radial tire expansion at its Gadsden, Alabama plant.''

And just as these are not isolated incidents, neither is corporate flight simply a result of poor economic conditions, or a trivial problem limited to a few old industrial towns in the "Frostbelt"—as some analysts would have the public believe.

The shocking fact is that between 1969 and 1976 at least *15 million jobs* were destroyed in the United States as a result of plant closings and shut-downs, an average of 2.1 million jobs each year. And the loss of each job is magnified by the negative effect on family and community—an effect rarely mentioned in corporate analyses of capital movement.

The business community usually tries to dismiss the problem with a few convenient assertions, such as:

• Capital movement is simply a regional problem, with limited impact on relatively small numbers of people.

• Unregulated capital mobility is both essential and beneficial to the economy as a whole.

• Tax incentives and other government payments to business will quickly correct any imbalances that exist.

Together these form an attractive mythology which obscures the truth.

It is important to replace these myths with a realistic—and unfortunately far more disturbing—picture. This true picture is of worldwide capital movement of enormous size and velocity, uncontrolled by any governmental efforts to mitigate its destructive effects.

TO DATE, the amount of disinvestment which has taken place in communities around the country—

both from one region to another and from America abroad—has been consistently and substantially underestimated. Not only are the methods which have been used to survey migrant businesses inaccurate, but they fail altogether to take account of more subtle forms of disinvestment than actual physical plant movement (the basis for most business estimates of impact). For example, a company may allow its facilities to deteriorate and use the savings (in the form of depreciation allowances) to reinvest in other branches, in other businesses, or in securities. Or a company might close an old facility and sell off its assets, or declare bankruptcy, and use the surplus money for a new economic activity or for pensions for its owner.

Another more subtle form of disinvestment which often occurs is the severe reduction of operations at an old facility by a multibranch corporation, which then gradually shifts machinery, skilled labor, managers, or marketing responsibilities to newer facilities elsewhere. Such a multibranch corporation may also leave an older plant's capital stock in place but simply reallocate the plant's profits to another, newer, facility. This "milking" of a profitable plant is especially common among conglomerates (where the term "cash cow" is sometimes used to describe the object of such a profit drain) and is responsible for ruining many sound companies. In fact, this last management technique (to be discussed further in this book) is one facet of an amazing corporate activity which occurs not infrequently: the shutting down of healthy, profitable plants—not just money-losers.

IT IS certainly true that a great deal of capital movement during the last few years has been region-to-region; the terms "Frostbelt" and "Sunbelt" have become part of a convenient shorthand to describe the well-publicized exodus of industry from the Northern tier of old industrial states to the warmer (and often union-free) environment of the Southern and Western states. In manufacturing industries especially, where organized labor has had its strongest roots, these shifts have been particularly dramatic: from 1960-1976, Southern manufacturing capital stock grew almost twice as fast as that of the Northeast, and 65 percent faster than in the North Central region.

If so much of the nation's new investment in plant is outside the Frostbelt, then job loss is sure to eventually follow. Indeed, between 1969 and 1976, Frostbelt firms destroyed about 111 jobs through plant closings for every 100 new jobs they created, while companies in the South and West shut down 80 jobs while opening 100. The heavy movement of capital out of the older cities of the North has clearly had great human cost—a cost businesses tend to ignore or minimize—but the Frostbelt-Sunbelt movement is not the whole story. In fact, there is now a great deal of evidence pointing to disinvestment from the *South as well,* jobs either lost or moved out of the country entirely. Surprisingly, the rate at which manufacturing plants have been closing is actually *higher* in the South than anywhere else; from 1969-1976, the odds that a plant which employed more than 100 workers in 1969 would be shut by 1976 were better than one in three in the South.

Part of what is happening in the South, thanks to the international growth of corporations (to be discussed later on), is the continuing movement of capital outside the U.S. Southern states would seem to be experiencing—in a much more compressed time period—the same "turnover" of capital (that is, capital proceeding through several stages of economic development) as the

North has experienced. For example, it took 75 years for the Northeast to lose the bulk of its old mill-based industry to the Sunbelt and to foreign countries. Yet already, within a much shorter time span, the South has witnessed the overseas migration of textiles, apparel, and other non-durables. To select just one industry, between 1971 and 1976 almost 60 percent of all textile mill closings—in both union and non-union plants—occurred in the South.

THE SHEER magnitude of capital movement overseas belies the corporate notion that disinvestment is only a regional problem. Since the end of World War II, the growth of American investment in other countries has been enormous: from 1950-1974, this foreign investment increased tenfold (from $11 billion to over $118 billion), a rate more than double that of gross private domestic investment.

This foreign investment has, as might be expected, a significant effect on employment in the United States. The U.S. Tariff Commission has reported that:

• When American firms both produce and sell their products abroad, they cut into the exports of firms operating in the U.S.

• Overseas operations usually rely to a greater extent on foreign-made intermediate goods.

• When American-made parts are assembled abroad and shipped back to the U.S. as a finished product—the so-called "export platform" or "offshore assembly" process—they displace workers who would otherwise have done assembly work in the U.S.

• When U.S. firms grant licenses to foreign firms for use of patented technology or production processes, the foreign firms can often in time displace the American firm on the world market and even inside the United

States—causing further elimination of American jobs.

This massive overseas investment is not just in automobiles, television sets and tape recorders; it is in food, clothing, drugs, forest products, transportation—almost any industry found in the U.S. During the decade 1957-1967, a third of all U.S. transportation equipment plants were located abroad, one-fourth of all chemical plants, one-fifth of machinery. For example: in 1966, as an alternative to expanding its older, unionized TV factory in Cincinnati, RCA opened a 4000-employee facility in Memphis. When the Memphis workers organized a union, RCA closed *both* plants and moved all of its black-and-white TV production to Taiwan.

The General Instrument Corporation, a New York-based firm that produces electronic equipment, employed 14,000 production and maintenance workers in the early 1960s in plants in Massachusetts, New Jersey, and eventually in Kentucky as well. By 1978, all of these plants had been closed, and the operations shifted to—once again—Taiwan.

During the 1960s, Litton Industries, a famous conglomerate, acquired Royal Typewriter. Over the next 15 years, domestic production was shifted from Hartford, Connecticut, to Springfield, Missouri, and then to Portugal and England, to get inside the Common Market tariff wall. This last move eliminated some 4,000 American jobs.

SOME COMPANIES specialize in buying small American firms only to close them down and take their machinery overseas, a practice that seems especially common in the shoe industry. American Shoe Machine Company, for example, purchased a modern U.S. factory, shut it down, and shipped the lasts, dies, patterns, management, and much of the leather to Europe, where it now makes shoes at 50 cents per hour, as compared to $3 per hour in the United States.

Another source of cheap labor is Mexico, which in 1965 initiated a program which allows foreign-owned companies to set up operations within a tax and tariff-free 12½ mile strip along Mexico's northern border. "Our idea is to offer an alternative to Hong Kong . . . " the Mexican Minister of Commerce told the *Wall Street Journal* (May 25, 1967). U.S. tariff code regulations allow U.S. corporations to import products assembled in that zone with minimal tax.

The growth of strikes and high turnover that result inevitably from monotonous and hazardous work caused many companies to move further south in the mid-1970s; Mexico obliged by opening three new tax and duty-free areas in the central part of the country. Most recently, Chrysler has used part of its well-publicized bail-out package to set up engine facilities in central Mexico. These engines will be shipped back into the U.S. to be installed on the new K-cars.

The long list of large American corporations which have closed American plants and moved jobs overseas includes Bulova, whose President has been quoted as saying, "We are able to beat the foreign competition because we *are* the foreign competition." Indeed, by the end of the 1970s, overseas profits accounted for a third or more of the overall profits of the hundred largest multinational producers and banks based in the United States. The growth in multinational banking activity is less frequently publicized than corporate flight, but is just as noteworthy: in 1964, only 11 U.S. banks operated foreign branches, with assets of only $7 billion. Eight years later, 107 banks had foreign assets of over $90 billion. And in 1974, the Bank of America made 39 percent of its net operating income from foreign activities, while Chase Manhattan made 49 percent and Citibank an astounding 60 percent.

THE SIZE of this overseas investment, and its possible impact on American workers and the American economy, have magnified the debate over the actual effects of such investment. The research department of the AFL-CIO has taken the position that jobs are in fact being destroyed, while the Emergency Committee for American Trade (the multinationals' chief lobbyist) has said that they are not.

The central question for both sides is what the multinationals would have done had they been prohibited from investing overseas. Assuming that they would have tried to export an equivalent volume of goods from their domestic bases, could they have succeeded? Or would foreign competitors have dominated their overseas market?

In their book *Global Reach,* Richard Barnet and Ronald Muller note that:

> The favorable studies of the companies assume that if a worker now employed by a global corporation were not working for the corporation, he would be unemployed. The labor studies assume, on the other hand, that he is infinitely employable in the United States if only the corporation will keep their capital in the country . . . But even assuming that all foreign investment is "defensive," there are ways to protect a market position other than building a factory in Taiwan. Companies could have put more money into research and development in the United States . . . We could also ask what would have happened to the U.S. employment picture if U.S. firms had not been so ready to sell off their comparative advantage to their competitors by licensing technology to them for quick profits.

Two Cornell economists, Robert Frank and Richard Freeman, have attempted to statistically sort out the answer to the puzzle: the net domestic employment and income effect of private direct foreign investment. They conclude that in 1970, the effect of the actual $10 billion in American foreign investment was an average domestic job loss of 160,000 jobs, and that wages and national income were also significantly lower than if an equivalent flow of capital had been invested domestically.

TO THOSE who argue that unregulated capital movement is a cornerstone of the American economy, and that the need for a company to change its location within the U.S. or even to cross its borders is a necessary part of their ability to do business, it is important to put the debate in another context.

Clearly capital mobility, *per se,* is not the enemy. In a world of growing material scarcity, resources must be allocated in a wise and thoughtful manner. This often calls for removing capital from some types of activity in order to use it more productively in others.

The real problem is the accelerating velocity of capital movement, and the fact that the very real social and economic devastation which this frenetic, unplanned, and abrupt reallocation of resources causes is rarely considered in the decisions of corporate managers.

The basic issue, then, is not how to stop capital movement. It is instead how to assure that this transfer of capital from one use or location to another will meet real human needs without disregarding the full impact of such decisions on people and their communities.

Chapter Two

THE REAL IMPACT

CAPITAL MOVEMENT and corporate flight are more, of course, than troublesome issues of economics and public policy. For millions of Americans and their communities they represent a human tragedy: jobs lost, family assets used up, mental and physical health threatened, lives destroyed.

Because corporate decisions to reinvest their assets are based on balance sheets and profit margins, the effects on the thousands of workers that each such decision produces can be obscured in a blizzard of numbers and financial strategies. Indeed, it is an unavoidable fact of modern economic life that whenever capital is moved—whether it is across continents or just across the street—there will always be some who will benefit, and others who will pay a price. However, it is all too often the unemployed worker who pays that price, and no corporate strategies can salve the human suffering and personal loss.

The damage which the movement of capital does to the lives of workers and the fabric of a community can appropriately be characterized as a kind of "social violence." It is seldom measured, or even very well documented: it tends to be submerged in Gross National Product figures and disguised by impersonal unemployment rates. And certainly this story of personal and social trauma is rarely told in corporate annual reports.

But social violence does occur with frightening regularity, and its story can be told. Perhaps the best place to start is with the most obvious effect of plant closings: job loss and long-term unemployment.

The fact is that (except perhaps in areas where other industry is booming) plant closings don't often produce short-term or what is called "frictional" unemployment. Rather they tend to produce long periods of displacement, which can be especially severe if the shutdown occurs during a recession when the competition for other jobs is fierce, or if it occurs in a small community where few other jobs exist. A recent report prepared for the Federal Trade Commission, surveying a history of plant closings, examined twelve of the most thoroughly researched cases and reported that "in all the studies reviewed the impact on the employees was severe." For example, ten months after Mack Truck's 1961 abandonment of its 2,700 employee assembly plant in Plainfield, New Jersey, 23 percent of its workforce were still without jobs well after unemployment benefits were exhausted. A similar proportion remained unemployed *two years* after the 1956 Packard plant shutdown involving 4,000 workers. Another third of the Packard workforce found jobs after the closing, but lost these within the first twenty-four months of the original plant shutdown. Having lost all their seniority, often amounting to ten years or more, these workers were more vulnerable to layoffs on their new job.

A RECESSION can make reemployment even more of a struggle. When Armour and Company closed its Oklahoma City meat-packing plant in July 1960, laying off four hundred of its workforce, 50 percent remained unemployed for at least six months. More recently, a study of the 1975 closing of a chemical company branch plant in Fall River, Massachusetts, showed that the average duration of subsequent unemployment was nearly 60 weeks, with some workers idled as much as three years. About four workers out of every ten found jobs only after their unemployment compensation had long been exhausted.

It should be noted that the crippling effects of plant closings often hit hardest among minorities; those industries experiencing the most shutdowns are frequently in

Employment Gained or Lost Through Start-Ups, Closings, and Relocations of Private Business Establishments in Selected States, 1969–1976

(Employment level in 1,000s of jobs)

State and Region	Jobs created	Jobs destroyed	Ratio of jobs destroyed to jobs created
"FROSTBELT"			
New England			
Massachusetts	446	500	1.13
Connecticut	211	238	1.13
Mid-Atlantic			
New York	1,087	1,494	1.37
Pennsylvania	827	865	1.05
East North Central			
Michigan	639	552	0.86
Ohio	789	720	0.91
West North Central			
Minnesota	249	243	0.98
Missouri	321	305	0.95
"SUNBELT"			
South Atlantic			
Georgia	594	416	0.70
North Carolina	372	374	1.01
East South Central			
Alabama	283	252	0.89
Tennessee	354	296	0.84
West South Central			
Louisiana	300	233	0.76
Texas	1,153	830	0.72
Mountain			
Arizona	141	125	0.89
Colorado	238	174	0.73
Pacific			
California	1,820	1,477	0.81
Washington	244	180	0.74
U.S. Total	16,200	15,000	0.92

central cities and are those employing relatively large concentrations of minorities. A study by the Ohio Public Interest Campaign of employment gains and losses during the 1960s concluded:

In every case where black workers are disproportionately represented in the workforce, there has been significant manufacturing job losses . . . In every case where there has been significant manufacturing job gains, black workers are disproportionately underrepresented.

Similarly, there are also severe dislocations among women workers in several industries, notably including textiles, apparel, and electronics.

U NEMPLOYMENT ITSELF is only one part of the picture of human costs. Another consideration is the quality of whatever new job the worker obtains, and its salary level. Not surprisingly, the same study for the Federal Trade Commission noted that, "On the whole, new jobs pay less than the old ones and are less satisfying." One national sample of displaced workers showed that three-fifths experienced a decline in the status level of their new jobs, a downward trend that was in fact most acute among professional and managerial workers.

And as for reemployment salary levels, some workers have particular difficulty, such as those in the better-paying and unionized meat-packing, auto, aerospace, and steel industries. A study based on social security data found that annual earnings loss ranged from less than 1 percent in the TV receiver industry to more than 46 percent in steel. Even after *six years,* some workers continued to suffer as much as an 18 percent loss in income from its original level.

Incredibly, many displaced workers lose not only their jobs: they lose their built-up pension rights as well. For example, in 1975 the Federal Reserve Bank of Boston revealed that only 38 percent of displaced shoeworkers in

Massachusetts received or still expected to receive the money to which they were entitled. This kind of abuse has been curbed somewhat by the Employee Retirement Income Security Act (ERISA), enacted in 1974, which regulates the handling of pension money; but large multi-branch corporations can still terminate a particular plant or division—a "partial termination," according to the U.S. Department of Labor—and not pay workers some of their rightful benefits.

THE FINANCIAL strain of long-term unemployment doesn't affect just workers, of course. While families who fall victim to brief periods of lost earnings are often able to sustain themselves through savings and unemployment insurance, the victims of plant closings often suffer a total depletion of family savings and assets, and even mortgage foreclosure and reliance on public welfare. Just as the Great Depression drove millions of families into poverty, an increasing number of workers and their families are in the same situation today as a result of corporate flight.

Certainly the loss of personal assets places families in an extraordinarily vulnerable position. When savings run out, people lose the ability to respond to short-run crises—an unexpected health problem, a casualty or fire loss, or even a minor auto accident—and it hurls the family over the brink of economic solvency. The trauma extends well beyond the bounds of household money matters, and can cause a range of real physical and mental health problems.

For example, research has shown that workers who lose their jobs (and often their health insurance) due to factory closure suffer increased blood pressure (hypertension) and abnormally high cholesterol and blood sugar levels—factors related to heart disease. Other disorders include ulcers, respiratory diseases, hyper-allergic reactions, headaches, stomach trouble, heavy drinking, and loss of appetite. Compounding these problems is the fact that their families often cannot maintain an adequate standard of health care, nutrition and even housing.

The impact of unemployment on what has been called "social trauma" has been studied by Professor M. Harvey Brenner of Johns Hopkins University. His shocking conclusion was that a one percent increase in the aggregate unemployment rate sustained over a period of six years was associated with:

- 37,000 deaths (including 20,000 cardiovascular deaths);
- 920 suicides;
- 650 homicides;
- 4,000 state mental hospital admissions; and
- 3,300 state prison admissions.

Even these statistics do not, however, tell the entire story of the social trauma created by plant shutdowns and other permanent layoffs. The suicide rate among workers laid off due to plant closings, for example, is higher than among any other group. When the Federal Mogul Corporation closed its roller bearing plant in Detroit, eight of the 2,000 affected workers took their own lives. If this ratio, one in 250, were to be applied to the number of actual shutdowns in New England between 1969 and 1976, there would have been 4,000 suicides. If it were applied to plant closings around the nation, the number of suicides at least partly induced by plant shutdowns would exceed the number of Americans killed in Vietnam.

Child and spouse abuse, aggression, loss of confidence and feelings of uselessness are also serious problems. Some workers even develop a "blaming the victim" syndrome, and begin to believe that the plant closing was their fault, and that they couldn't hold a new job even if they found one. Such disturbances reflect the fact that plant closings deprive people of the structure by which they hold their communities together. A factory, particularly if it is the major institution in town, is thought of as community property. It is not only the means by which people meet their economic needs; it is also a social and cultural basis for their lives.

THE SOCIAL violence caused by plant closings is not limited just to workers and their families. Each dislocation has a "ripple effect" which can produce increased vulnerability for businesses that remain in the area, a weakened tax base and social infrastructure, and a higher incidence of crime. Some of these effects of capital flight may dissipate in time, especially if the local economy is expanding, but others may become a permanent part of the community's social and economic life.

When a large cutlery manufacturer, J. Wiss & Son, was acquired by a Texas conglomerate and relocated from Newark, New Jersey to North Carolina, the loss of 725 direct manufacturing jobs also cost the city 468 jobs "in stores, banks, bus service, luncheonettes, taverns, gas stations, and other local business," according to the New Jersey State AFL-CIO. Fourteen million dollars in purchasing power was removed from the local economy, half of which had resided in local banks.

The U.S. Department of Transportation (DOT), in a study of the likely effects of a shutdown of the Chrysler Corporation, estimated in 1979 that unemployment in the Detroit metropolitan area would climb swiftly to 16 to 19 percent (from 8.7 percent), and that on top of 170,000 auto plant jobs, another 192,000 jobs would be lost in firms that supply parts and services. By late 1980,

Chrysler had cut back its labor force to 80,000 and Detroit's unemployment rate rose above 20 percent, exceeding even DOT's dire predictions. At the very center of the dislocation were Detroit's racial minorities, whose workers not only lost thousands of jobs, but whose programs and services were most vulnerable to decreases in local tax revenue.

This loss of tax revenue is still another serious community effect of plant closings. It was forecast that in the first 39 months following the shutdown of the Youngstown Sheet and Tube mill in Campbell, Ohio, the total tax loss would be over $30 million; a total shutdown of the Chrysler Corporation might well cut off *half a billion dollars* in annual federal, state, and local income taxes normally paid by workers at Chrysler and associated businesses. The State of Massachusetts has developed a rule of thumb which says that every $10,000 salary-level job lost costs the region about $1,300 in state and local taxes.

As a result of these losses, just when a community faces the need to expand services to displaced workers, its tax base falls apart. Local programs and services face severe cuts, and public employees—including police and firefighters—also face layoffs.

THERE ARE many other profound effects of plant closings, ones which are more difficult to measure. One effect is a change in the status of other workers in the community not directly affected by the shutdown. When GAF closed a plant in Binghamton, New York, one study has shown, "Local union leadership felt that the uncertainty regarding GAF's future, and a pool of 1,100 potential strikebreakers in the displacees, severely constrained its ability to strike successfully," and even to negotiate. Another problem has been blacklisting of workers: when the Brockway motor truck company closed in Cortland, New York, employers were reluctant to hire its people, who were accustomed to high wages and union benefits. At the same time, the community felt that the union militancy and bargaining demands were the reason that the plant had closed. Indeed there is a growing trend to use trade unionism itself as a scapegoat to hide the real causes of plant closings.

One of these is the spread of absentee ownership and "remote control" of local economic activity. A chilling fact which lies in the background of the dislocation problem but is of no small significance is the large percentage of shutdowns which are ordered by corporations headquartered in communities other than the one affected. It is part of the increasing centralization of economic decision-making which, according to a 1976 study, has resulted in 80 percent of the states in the U.S. (notably including much of the Sunbelt) experiencing an "outward shift" in corporate control of local economies.

What makes this so critical is that absentee control can affect a local business community even without a traumatic plant closing. For instance the parent firm might reorganize secondary business relationships, and require its subsidiary to give up local legal help, suppliers, accountants, and so on, in favor of those chosen by the parent. There are also political implications of outside ownership. Local managers of absentee-owned corporations are usually powerful actors in local politics, and on industrial relations issues, particularly in state legislatures. Even so, their real commitment to the community may be tenuous at best. Communities have difficulty holding these managers accountable, because of course they take orders from corporate headquarters, and must place the interests of the corporation ahead of the community if they are to keep their positions. As a consequence, one study maintains that, as a "general rule . . . the sale of factories to outside interests dampens the possibilities for progressive economic or civic planning within states or communities."

All of this increases the economic vulnerability of the community, and certainly creates a psychology of uncertainty and diminished control over local political life.

W HAT IS most surprising, perhaps, is that the social violence of dislocation is not confined simply to communities where plants have closed. Many defenders of unrestrained capital mobility say that for every victim of a plant closing there is a person who benefits from the influx of capital into a new area. Theoretically, at least, the two balance out. Unfortunately, in practice the two assumptions inherent in this notion are both false. First, the victims are not compensated by the gainers because our mechanisms for redistributing good fortune are poorly developed. Second, the rapid growth created by new capital is often damaging in itself; along with new jobs come overcrowded schools, higher taxes and property values, and increased crime. And all are compounded by the loss of local political control.

Houston, for example, is one of this nation's fastest growing cities. It looks and feels vibrant; banks and multinational corporations find its cheap energy and low taxes attractive. But the city's rapid growth has taken place at the expense of zoning or any other kind of planning, and as a result it suffers from highway congestion, air pollution, water shortages, and a housing crisis which has 29 percent of the poor living in substandard dwellings. There is an astonishing disparity between rich and poor, with the poor having an infant mortality rate "that would," according to one college professor, "have embarrassed the Belgian Congo." In Houston and other "boomtowns," the effect of a massive influx of capital is the creation of a permanent underclass and the trauma of a "dual" economy: in Houston the murder rate is 18 killings per 100,000 residents, one of the highest in the nation.

With anarchic hyper-investment and unplanned growth, a "boomtown/busttown" phenomenon is developing in many of our cities. As a result, a large number of the so-called "winners" of the Sunbelt join the "losers" of the Frostbelt as victims in the frantic race of capital from one area to another.

Chapter Three

THE NEW ERA OF FLIGHT— AND FIGHT

WHAT HAS changed significantly in the last several decades is not the *willingness* of business to move its capital and assets, but its *ability* to do so. Indeed, successful entrepreneurship has always rested to some extent on responding to the need for change—to get in or out of a particular product, service, or location—to improve a company's fortunes.

During the several decades since the Second World War many of the constraints on such changes have been relaxed, and at the same time there has been a dramatic increase in the competitive pressures on business to move their assets around in order to squeeze out the last ounce of profit—often rapidly and in staggering amounts. The unprecedented size and velocity of this capital transfer too frequently results in shattered lives and communities torn apart.

The inescapable reality is that the new mobility of capital has changed the rules of the game for management and labor, and management is moving both to consolidate its gains and to press its advantage. Not only are corporations using the threat of flight to win concessions from workers and tax giveaways from localities, but now they are also standing to fight, to slug it out with unions and government over issues like business regulation, unemployment compensation and public services. Corporations are flexing their immense economic and political muscles, and they are getting stronger—and winning more and more. To understand why the rules have changed, and why capital is now moving so rapidly between states and between countries, it's necessary to look at a little history, and at some changing conditions that have set the stage.

THE TENDENCY toward the centralization of power and control in the hands of multiplant, multiregional, and multinational corporations is at the heart of the new capital mobility. Although there are still many more small businesses than large ones, the corner grocery store, hardware store, and the one-person real estate agency now exist only on the margins of our economy. All are being replaced by their conglomerate counterparts. The last few decades have brought massive concentration of economic power—by 1972, for example, the "Big Three" automakers produced 93 percent of U.S. cars, and a "Big Four" were responsible for 90 percent of all breakfast cereal. Along with their economic power goes political power, and the result is that the small groups of directors of such companies not only can make reinvestment decisions in relative secrecy, but that they are often not answerable for the disruption they cause, either in the marketplace or in the political arena.

A major factor in this concentration was that until quite recently, the freedom to locate production was tightly constrained by the available network of transportation and communication. Producers had to be close to either their consumers or their suppliers: moving goods on a large scale took too long and cost too much to keep profits healthy.

The introduction of the railroad and a modern highway system significantly reduced the time, and thus the cost, and began to pave the way for capital migration. For instance, the South was opened to production facilities even while the Northern and Mid-Western states remained the major markets for consumer products. By 1925 most of the textile spindleage in the U.S. was located in the South.

Air travel and the telephone allowed production to take place even further from consumer and supplier markets, and now the extensive use of the computer and high-speed telecommunications allow managers in a corporation's headquarters to closely control production and sales anywhere in the world.

What is called the "product cycle" also plays a key role in facilitating the new capital mobility. As a new industry matures, for those processes of production which managers can make routine, actual manufacture need no longer be located near centers of innovation or in places where highly skilled labor is available. Again, the textile industry is a good example: when the basics of the automated loom had been perfected by the early twentieth century, innovation—and thus the need to be close to sources of technical expertise—weakened. Shifting production facilities to the South to use unorganized, low-wage labor became both possible and profitable. Computer companies, to take another obvious example, began to move many of their factories to Ireland, Latin America and Asia once the technology for semiconductors, magnetic cores, and memory chips became sufficiently routine.

Such advances are not simply the result of random technological experimentation; high technology is simply too expensive to develop without explicit reason. In fact, corporate managers have actively searched for ways to be free of limitations: wide-bodied cargo aircraft were developed to accommodate rapid movement of high value cargo, while much computer technology was created specifically to coordinate the widespread activities of multinational corporations. Moreover, the ability of industry to encourage and take advantage of new technology has been increased manifold by the radical changes in the organizational structure of American business since the nineteenth century. The control of a greater and greater share of productive capacity by corporations and conglomerates makes it possible for business to take advantage of the technological advances that speed capital mobility.

SIMPLE ELIMINATION of competition was the impetus for the first wave of births of giant U.S. corporations that took place at the turn of the century. Then from the mid-1920s into the mid-1930s, the trend toward concentration took the form of large firms absorbing their suppliers or distributors, or both, with the financial backing for these vertical combinations coming from investment banking houses. During these years the major oil companies emerged, using networks of wholly-owned or franchised small companies to control the petroleum industry, from drilling through refining to the retail sale of gasoline.

The modern conglomerate movement—consisting of companies whose fundamental business activities are buying and selling other companies, not necessarily in related product areas—began with the creation of Textron Inc. during World War II, and multiplied rapidly. By the late 1960s, more than four-fifths of all corporate mergers were conglomerate in nature; between 1967 and 1969, an annual average of 3500 businesses were swallowed up in this way. According to the U.S. Federal Trade Commission, the number of mergers and takeovers of $100-million companies has increased by 500 percent since 1975.

The most aggressive acquirers are now those corporations with huge amounts of cash to invest and which are under intense competitive pressure to extend their international and inter-industry control. Not surprisingly, oil companies head the list: in 1976, Mobil Oil purchased the Marcor Corporation, which was itself the result of a merger between Montgomery Ward and the Container Corporation of America. And in 1979, the world's largest oil company, Exxon, acquired the Reliance Electric Company, the nation's third largest manufacturer of electric motors.

Unfortunately, conglomeration usually creates little or no new productive capacity: the capital invested amounts to only a shifting of assets from one organization to another, not the building of new employment opportunities. And the "increased efficiency" and "rationalization" of the operation of widespread businesses which is usually heralded as a principal benefit of mergers is in fact something of a myth. Often the result is duplication of services and functions and great inefficiency; for acquired companies whose assets are drained off, the result—which we can see with alarming frequency—is a rapid decline in profitability and a sudden sale or shutdown.

ANOTHER POPULAR myth, used repeatedly by conservatives to encourage opposition to governmental regulation or taxation of corporations, is that the ownership of American companies is distributed widely among millions of ordinary working Americans who are stockholders. In fact, individuals have been net sellers of stock for about 20 years; nearly three-quarters of the trading done on the New York Stock Exchange is done by institutions. In the early 1970s, individuals made equity investments averaging about $100 million per year, while banks and insurance companies were investing between $4 *billion* and $14 *billion*.

This growing influence of financial institutions in the concentration of corporate power has come about through trust department purchases of stock and corporate bonds. For example, Chase Manhattan Bank is now the single largest shareholder in General Electric, Union Carbide, Atlantic Richfield, AT&T, and several airlines, as Citibank is for Xerox, Bendix, Kraft Foods and Pennzoil. The House Judiciary Committee acknowledged this trend in 1971, publicly stating that banks were indeed promoting corporate and conglomerate mergers.

BIG BANKS are not alone in promoting concentration and centralization. The government itself, through tax and tariff policies and through regulation (and non-regulation), has acted to encourage and protect concentrated economic power and conglomeration. A study by the FTC concluded that the U.S. Tax Code encouraged capital investment through accelerated depreciation allowances, which essentially give companies interest-free government loans; investment tax credits, which allow deferral of a portion of the tax indefinitely and thus for some companies approach total tax forgiveness; and mineral resource (notably oil) depletion allowances, which end up paying for the cost of drilling the original hole in the ground. The resulting estimated cost to the taxpayers in foregone Treasury revenues was $10.9 billion in 1978 alone. The problem is that most of these benefits went disproportionately to the largest corporations.

The tax code benefits conglomerates most of all. For example, they often can use "creative" accounting procedures to artificially enhance the value of their subsidiaries, thus deducting heavily for their operating costs at the same time they may be milking them of their profits. As the value of assets are inflated, earnings per share and stock prices go up—and the proceeds from the sale of inflated stock can then be used to acquire more companies.

Of course, such a pyramid can collapse when the inflated stock no longer sells; the conglomerate has to rely on the profits of its subsidiaries for new cash, and finds that the lifeblood has been drained from once sound companies.

Unhappily, this kind of dangerous behavior most often is overlooked by regulatory agencies, much less challenged. Litigation is expensive and time-consuming, and few public officials have the stamina to stay with it. Of the 14,000 mergers that took place between 1950 and 1967, fewer than 200 were challenged, and although the government won 90 of those cases, only 48 companies were required to divest themselves of anything—less than *one-half of one percent* of the original mergers.

THE PHENOMENAL growth of multinational corporations and conglomerates has been stimulated by more than U.S. tax or regulatory policies, and by more than structural changes in the American economy: it has also shaped, and been shaped by, fundamental changes in *international* economic relations. These trends have also led to rapid capital movement and its consequences for the U.S. labor force.

For the two decades after World War II, the movement of American capital into world markets paralleled the rise of the United States as the dominant force in the political, economic, and military world order. Western Europe and Japan spent much of that period rebuilding war-shattered economies. As a result, they were almost completely dependent on the United States for imports, particularly of capital goods. American corporations acquired vast assets overseas, and opened profitable new markets. In the course of this worldwide expansion, American firms also began to transfer assets abroad to establish production facilities that directly competed with facilities and employment in this country.

In 1945, the future in Europe and elsewhere for American business looked rosy. The Bretton Woods conference had in the year before established the dollar as the primary currency of the Western world, and foreign banks were required to use their currencies to purchase excess dollars, giving U.S. companies the francs, marks, and pounds with which to pay for foreign production sites. Foreign banks were placed in the uncomfortable position of helping to finance the American takeover of their own nation's industries.

The overseas profits of U.S. corporations rose steadily from about 10 percent of their total after-tax profits in the early 1950s to about 20 percent in the 1970s. And overseas investment became increasingly attractive as U.S. tax and tariff regulations were rewritten. The tax code now permits U.S. companies to credit all of their foreign income taxes against their tax liabilities at home, on a dollar for dollar basis—providing a far greater savings than is normally available on other business expenses. U.S. firms also can defer payment of taxes in the U.S. until profits are actually repatriated, a bonus that enables corporations to manipulate their accounting procedures to keep profits circulating abroad and thus never subject to U.S. taxes. As a part of this complex process, a U.S. parent firm may, for example, engage in what is called "transfer pricing": setting an arbitrarily high price for an item or service it sells to its own overseas subsidiary, thereby manipulating to their own tax advantage the profits they earn in each country.

These and other tax breaks contributed to the startling fact that, in 1972 for example, American corporations paid only $1.2 billion in taxes to the U.S. government on foreign earnings of over $24 billion. More than any other single factor, these tax "incentives" for foreign investment were responsible for the decline of the effective federal income tax rate paid by U.S. corporations from 51 percent in 1960 to 28 percent in 1974.

The Tariff Code also favors overseas investments by limiting the amount of duty that must be paid on

foreign-made products. This has contributed to the phenomenal growth of "export platforming," whereby American firms manufacture components in the U.S., ship them to low-wage European and Third World countries for assembly, and import them back into the U.S. for domestic sale. Duty is paid only on the value added in the foreign assembly process, rather than on the entire market value of the assembled product. Recent revisions of tariff laws have removed even the requirement that there be token final processing in the U.S. The beneficiaries of this policy now include manufacturers of aircraft parts, steel mill products, semiconductors, textiles, apparel, televisions and radios. Yet with all of this capital shifted into foreign production, there is unfortunately no real evidence that American workers ultimately benefit from the availability of consumer goods at lower prices—the standard argument usually put forward by business economists.

THE RAPID expansion of American corporate investment overseas—helped along by tax and tariff policies as well as the manipulation of governmental fiscal and monetary policies to bolster the steady growth of aggregate demand—began to unravel in the 1960s. American military and political hegemony began to decline, as did American preeminence in productive capacity and technological innovation. The era of unprecedented growth formally ended in 1971, with the decision of the Nixon Administration to float the dollar and free it from the 25-year regime of fixed currency exchange rates to which it had been both anchor and base. With this erosion of the prominent international position of U.S. enterprise, Japanese and European competitors (many of them state-owned) arose in one industry after another, including steel, rubber, textiles, automobiles and electronics.

Surprisingly, some activities of U.S. multinationals have actually encouraged this foreign competition. American business has often gained access to foreign markets by licensing foreign firms to use American technology (for a royalty) or have agreed to joint production arrangements, sometimes involving the construction of a "turnkey" plant which is subsequently sold to the host country for a profit. In both cases, short-term corporate policy is helping to create its own future competition.

Co-production agreements—in which U.S. firms contract with foreign firms to produce a portion of a given product—have become a fact of corporate life, especially in the aircraft, electronics, and now the automobile industries. Occasionally such agreements are thrust on a U.S. company as an unattractive but unavoidable condition of doing business (as in the sale of U.S. aircraft overseas), but more often they serve to provide the U.S. company with access to large pools of cheap labor—in return for American technical expertise.

Indeed, the search for cheap labor all over the world will only intensify in the years ahead. Even as they cooperate on the supply side of international production, U.S. companies are forced to go head-to-head with their overseas competitors to gain every possible advantage and maintain their profits. Added to their problems in finding ever-cheaper labor is the growing resistance, especially by nationalist movements in the Third World, to exploitation by multinationals. This element in combination with an already unstable international political picture creates a period of economic uncertainty and heightened competition. Even *Business Week* is distressed at the bleak picture, as they noted in July of 1979:

The cooperative effort to create an interdependent world economy—hallmark of the postwar period—is being replaced by what often appears to be a free-for-all among industrial nations trying to grab or preserve as much as possible for themselves of the shrinking economic pie.

To be sure, the competition is becoming desperate, and consequently not even revolution and nascent nationalism has discouraged American investment in Third World countries. From 1969 to 1973 real manufacturing output in the Third World grew nearly twice as fast as in the United States, Europe, and Japan. And in 1976, while the U.S. exported $115 billion in merchandise, majority-owned foreign affiliates of U.S. corporations exported $144 billion.

The changes in international trading patterns brought on by this corporate activity have helped to produce a new situation for Americans at home. As Richard Barnet and Ronald Muller point out in *Global Reach,* the U.S. now exports increasing amounts of agricultural products in order to earn the foreign exchange to buy energy and raw materials, as well as consumer goods which are manufactured abroad. This then produces food shortages and rising food prices at home.

O F COURSE, business does not propose that its movement of assets and facilities is merely done to pursue cheap labor both domestically and worldwide. Rather it offers other explanations, and, indeed, the real reasons for corporate flight are somewhat more complex—if different from what management suggests.

Most orthodox analysts theorize that investment decisions are based on management's meticulous examination of the relative costs of doing business in alternative locations, and choosing those sites which minimize costs (assuming that markets are available for the firm's products or service). According to this theory, plants will be located where the sum total of costs—including wages, energy, land acquisitions, raw material costs, finance costs, and the level of taxes—is lowest. It follows that those communities which offer the least-cost package of inputs will attract capital from higher-cost areas.

Although there are factors that this framework neglects, such as unionization, there is clearly a fundamental logic to the explanation. And there is also some evidence to support the least-cost notion. Yet more careful examination suggests that the theory is inadequate.

Differences in transportation costs might account for a "city versus suburbs" decision, but there do not appear to be any particular regional differences in such costs (at least within the continental U.S.); similarly, land costs also appear to vary most between the city and its environs, and not between North and South. As the availability of large-scale and low-cost transportation increases, proximity to raw materials decreases as a location determinant—with the possible exception of energy costs.

Indeed, energy costs *do* vary widely between regions, and although such costs do not now appear to play a significant role in location decisions, should states rich in oil and gas decide to use their energy royalties to cut back or abolish all state and local taxes, energy costs might very well become a prime factor in capital movement. States like Alaska, Texas, and Louisiana will be the big gainers.

Certainly direct labor costs do play a role in location decisions. But when wage rates are put together with productivity to calculate unit labor costs, no one region of the country enjoys a clear advantage across all industrial sectors; rather, certain regions have lower unit costs in certain industries. Evidence suggests that firms in labor-intensive industries, then, may well try to move to lower unit labor costs. And by far the lowest labor costs are located outside the United States. Whereas labor costs might vary by ten percent between regions within the United States, the variation between the U.S. and the Third World might be eight or nine *hundred percent*!

EVEN SO, business trends to emphasize other factors as the primary determinants in location decisions, including an amorphous concept commonly referred to as the "business climate." If much of the industry-sponsored advertising is to be believed, a good business climate—meaning a pro-business government stand on regulation and taxation—is a more important part of the location decision than wages, energy costs, or anything else. And it would seem that states have taken the bait: tens of millions of dollars are spent each year to convince footloose industry that the state doing the hustling is the best place for business.

The business climate explanation of plant location rests on two basic principles: first, that regulations, taxes, and social welfare expenditures entail direct costs to industry, providing strong incentive for firms to locate where these costs are minimal; second, that the "social wage"—that package of non-wage benefits which governments provide to workers in order to maintain their health and purchasing power when they are unable to work—entails (along with certain types of regulations) indirect costs to business, in that they tend to affect the prices of other inputs, including labor, energy, and waste disposal rights.

On both counts states are trying hard to lure industry by providing a "healthy" business climate and a willing

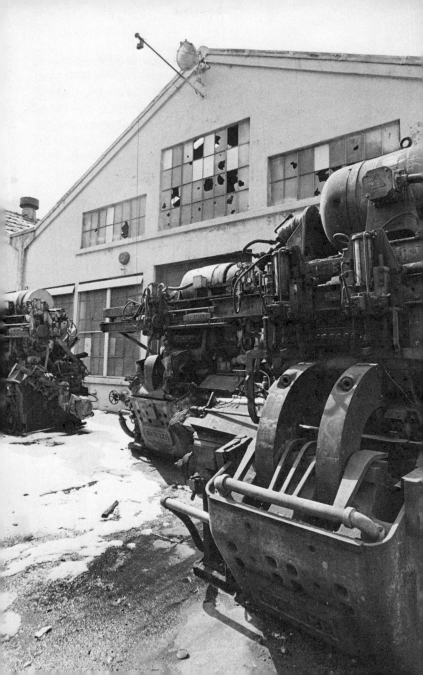

work force. The regulatory targets include governmental efforts—particularly widespread since the 1960s—to reduce the health and safety hazards and other social costs of economic development, to improve the planning of individual communities, and to control resource use and pollution. Management's strategy centers on portraying the regulatory system as procedurally unmanageable and too costly (to business) for the benefits it provides.

The bite of taxation—at federal, state, and local levels—has long been a favorite complaint of business, ostensibly choking off investment and forcing capital to move to lightly taxed regions. For example, the combination of higher wages and taxes has frequently been cited as responsible for the movement of industry out of the Frostbelt, and corporate lobbyists continue to press for tax relief and tax incentives using the argument that "high tax" states cannot effectively compete for jobs with their more pro-business neighbors.

The struggle between management and labor over the social wage has continued for decades. But it is not so much that the social wage directly affects the cost of doing business, as it is that it also protects workers from the full impact of unemployment and provides unorganized workers with some defense against the power of employers. The long-standing resistance of Southern (and some Western) states to raising the social wage has produced striking interregional differences in workers' standards of living. Now it is commonplace for corporate interests, through groups like the Chamber of Commerce and the National Association of Manufacturers, to pressure the high social wage states to provide better business climates—by freezing or actually lowering social services, income supports, and other institutional safeguards won by labor.

The frequency and stridency of current promotion notwithstanding, there would appear to be less to the business climate location theory than meets the eye. Several statistical studies have concluded that there is little evidence to support the notion that a so-called favorable business climate will actually stimulate locational activity. This is particularly true in the context of tax incentives, discussed in the following chapter. Not only do some businesses appear to distrust extraordinary concessions—figuring that they may be camouflaging some more serious problems—but clearly most large corporations, rather than being attracted to a good business climate, make locational decisions for other reasons, and only then use their immense political and economic power to *create* a good business climate for themselves. Especially where workers and communities are poorly organized, where unions are inactive or under attack, firms will generally have little trouble manipulating regulations, taxes, and the social wage to their advantage.

A MORE accurate analysis of the complex circumstances of business location should look behind the business climate argument to a stronger—if indeed much less publicized—motive for management. That is simply that capital is running away from labor unions. The new corporate agenda with respect to organized labor exists on two levels: first, a great deal of evidence—even from the business press—indicates that the Frostbelt-Sunbelt shift is largely a response to unions and labor activity in the North; second, in the world economy, multinational corporations are attempting to reorganize the international division of labor in order to play off workers of one nation against those of another.

Indeed, unions (when they are doing their job) *do* get in the way of management, by resisting arbitrary control over the production process by employers and by fighting actively for the rights and interests of workers—occasionally by way of strikes. Although management is usually reluctant to publicly attack unions, business is steadily increasing the size and scope of its union-busting activities. As Ron Chernow reports in *Working Papers,* "spearheading management's new militance is a growing industry of professional union-busters who have steamlined the art and given it a new elan that blends with the conservatism of the 1980s. In place of old-fashioned goons are legions of industrial psychologists, personnel managers, and labor lawyers . . ." A New England business journal portrayed Vermont as offering the signal asset of "a docile, effective work force" with little union activity.

The antipathy to unions is so great in some places in the South that companies in highly-unionized industries are actively discouraged from moving in, even if they are bringing new jobs.

Besides the new technology and sophistication of professional union-busters, management is now armed with other effective weapons. "Parallel production"—the creation of duplicate production facilities in different locations—is particularly common when the first facility is a union shop. Similarly, union activity in the constellation of smaller suppliers that serve large corporations can be effectively discouraged by "second-sourcing," when the purchasing corporation plays off suppliers against each other by refusing to grant sole source arrangements, even to subcontractors who might offer a slight competitive advantage.

There can also be little doubt that a good deal of the massive shift of corporate activity in the 1960s and 1970s from the United States to Europe, Canada, Japan, the Far East, and the Third World represents a concrete response to the very presence—and occasional disruptive behavior—of American industrial unions. However, corporate strategy has now become more complex and sophisticated than simple "flight" from unions. Through the development of parallel production in two or more different countries, and other tactics, corporations can play the labor force of one country against others, and keep unions (especially those back in the U.S.) on the defensive. The recent development and marketing of what is being called the "world car" is the most striking example of this reorganization. The Ford "Fiesta" is built with parallel production of most components, and is a direct result of Ford's efforts to reduce its vulnerability to labor disruption. Interestingly, because Ford is still somewhat vulnerable at the assembly stage of the Fiesta, the company is experimenting with the introduction of computer-controlled robots on the assembly line.

J UST AS management has introduced radically new production techniques in its efforts to find and retain cheap labor and avoid union activity, the last few years have also witnessed significant changes in what management views as its central operating objectives, and the criteria it uses for evaluating corporate performance. For example, there is now a great deal of evidence that many companies which are divisions or subsidiaries of large corporations and conglomerates are routinely required to meet annual profit targets, often described as "hurdle rates." Failure to achieve the target rate of return, which frequently is over 20 percent, can mean that the subsidiary is sold—or worse, is shut down. In fact, there are a number of examples of healthy, profitable companies whose profits did not meet the necessary "hurdle rate" and who were then closed, throwing their employees out of work and their communities into turmoil. The *Wall Street Journal* in March of 1978 reported that the Uniroyal Corporation had chosen to close an inner tube plant in Indianapolis because of "steadily declining demand" and "high labor costs." But the real story was that the profitable

plant was simply not making *enough* of a profit for management. Fortunately, the workers, with the help of the community and their union, were able to purchase the plant themselves. Six hundred jobs were saved, and the plant still makes a profit.

Another management variation on the same theme is the siphoning off of subsidiaries' profits back to the

parent corporation, to reallocate according to the home office's priorities. This can create a severe structural imbalance in the subsidiary's operations: in good years, the profits go to the parent, and in poor years, the subsidiary has been stripped of its reserves and left to hope for refinancing from the parent or some other source.

Frequently conglomerates have tended to place the capital obtained from their subsidiaries into totally unrelated operations, instead of reinvesting in the same sector. American steel companies—which are now complaining loudly about their competitive disadvantage caused by outdated equipment and plant—have been guilty of this kind of investment strategy for a number of years and are now paying (or, indeed, are asking the taxpayer to pay) the price. According to the corporate reports of United States Steel, the share of that corporation's annual plant and equipment investment going into the production of steel *per se* fell from 69 percent in 1976 to just over half in 1979. In fact, in 1978, 44 percent of the corporation's worldwide assets were in non-steel businesses.

The dramatic and well-publicized closing of the Youngstown Sheet and Tube Company in 1977 is another sad example of the same management technique. Before its acquisition in 1969 by a small conglomerate, the Lykes Corporation, Sheet and Tube averaged $10 million per year in investment in plant and equipment. After acquisition, the average fell to $3 million, and would have been close to zero without a few investment projects quickly abandoned in the 1975-76 recession.

The "remote control" over subsidiaries' operations exerted by a corporate home office can have other undesirable effects. The home office can, for example, require its branches to carry redundant personnel, absorb part of the overhead of the parent, or purchase inputs from distant suppliers having a relationship with the parent.

The conventional wisdom that highly centralized corporations have brought a higher degree in managerial and operational efficiency in recent years may be well off the mark as well; large corporations are in fact often *creating* inefficiencies by over-management (usually in pursuit of short-term profits at the expense of the company's—or the workers'—future), milking subsidiaries of their profits (the "cash cow" technique mentioned elsewhere), subjecting subsidiaries to unrealistic performance targets (and then frequently closing still-profitable plants to pursue other profit opportunities), and of course the greatest inefficiency of all for society: throwing hundreds of workers out of work unnecessarily, disrupting their lives and their communities.

Nonetheless, management shows no signs of changing its course. The stakes of international competition have never been higher, and business has a new determination—reinforced by a sympathetic administration—to move aside any obstacles in their march toward higher profits. It is clearly time for labor to organize and respond.

Chapter Four

WHAT'S WRONG WITH WITH PRESENT POLICIES?

EVEN IF most public officials and workers agree—as seems to be increasingly the case—that corporate flight and the new era of unrestrained capital mobility pose problems that demand action, the policies in evidence are failing.

In fact, it is probably not too far off to say that public responses to date have been to invoke the wrong policies for the wrong reasons, producing precisely the opposite of the desired effects.

To be sure, state legislators worry about the drain of capital from their regions, mayors struggle with their eroding tax base, trade unionists unhappily contemplate greater unemployment, and workers ponder uncertain futures and their families' well-being. But for all of this growing concern, there is little agreement on what should be done. As a result, public policies now fall mainly into two unhappy categories: misguided business incentives and supports enacted by state and local governments in a frantic effort to attract or hold capital; and a few inadequate welfare-type policies for dislocated workers.

Certainly no state representative or city council member likes to contemplate the possibility of a plant closing in their area, jolting the economic and social fabric of the community. And certainly the prospect of attracting new capital and new jobs is a worthy goal.

So as states and communities search desperately for ways to both slow the exodus of capital and attract new investment, they join a virtual stampede of jurisdictions across the country which are adopting business subsidies and tax abatement schemes in the belief that these are necessary both to lure new employers and retain those companies they already have. Needless to say, one result is intense competition for the same capital; *Business Week* in fact calls this situation "the Second War Between the States."

PUBLIC AID to the private sector is not a new phenomenon—it's been around in one form or another almost as long as the republic—but what is new is the size of these subsidies and the rate at which they are being granted. State and local governments are now showering on business a veritable storm of tax credits, abatements, subsidized loans, and development grants, and this is not all of the story. Relaxing regulation of business and limiting "social wage" legislation are seen as attractive companion policies which help to form a "good business climate," as was discussed in the previous chapter. Prime targets include environmental protection laws, occupational health and safety regulations, zoning statutes, building codes and anti-discrimination measures. Moreover there is pressure to hold down the social wage by pushing back efforts at progressive tax reform, restricting unemployment and workmen's compensation eligibility, lowering the minimum wage, and defeating labor law reform.

Enactment of these kinds of incentives for business often place workers in an uncomfortable, ironic position: lowering the social wage, shifting tax burdens away from corporations (on to the workers themselves) and outright subsidies all are promoted in the name of attracting and keeping jobs. Workers thus have the difficult choice of reinforcing these efforts by foregoing many of their hard-won benefits—in hopes of holding on to their jobs—or they can keep up the fight for better conditions and benefits—and risk watching their employer leave town, or build his next plant somewhere else.

State and local governments, while recognizing that industrial location decisions are influenced by a host of factors, have largely settled on tax and finance schemes as the way they can best have *direct* input into corporate behavior. And these schemes are highly visible: ads touting the unique benefits of one state or another appear everywhere, from magazines to airports. The new war between the states has become so widespread that a recent issue of *Fortune* ran promotional ads for no less than nineteen states and cities in a single issue!

BUSINESS SUBSIDIES from state and local governments fall into four principal categories: industrial development bonds (IDBs), tax breaks, loans and loan guarantees, and outright grants.

IDBs take advantage of a state's power to issue tax-exempt bonds, and thus can be used to raise finance capital more cheaply than most corporations can on their own. Their use caught on in the early 1960s and spread rapidly throughout the country. While only $20 million worth of IDBs were issued in 1958, the amount doubled every year to reach a total of over $1.8 *billion* ten years later. Although the federal government finally moved to limit the tax loss in 1968 by restricting the tax exemption on these bonds to $1 million per issue, pollution control bonds were exempted from the legislation. By 1977, over $3.5 billion in tax free securities had been issued, with the bulk of these bonds—nearly $3 billion worth—being pollution control related.

Tax breaks are most frequently associated with interstate rivalry. Exemptions from local property taxes (typically referred to as tax abatements) can take the form of a total tax "holiday" or a reduction in the assessed property value for a given number of years. Other forms of tax breaks include: personal income tax exemptions (especially for company executives), excise tax exemptions, moratoria on the taxation of machinery and raw material purchases, special accelerated depreciation allowances on capital equipment, and the elim-

ination of industrial sales tax liability.

These tax breaks can be expensive indeed. In 1977 New York City exempted $461 million in properties from nearly $54 million in taxes. The package of tax incentives for Massachusetts in 1975 cost over $80 million. Of this total, a 3 percent tax credit for the purchase of buildings and machinery cost the Commonwealth $18 million in foregone revenue; a rollback on tangible property taxes cost another $25 million; and sales tax exemptions lost the state treasury $25 million more.

To take another incentive vehicle, at least fifteen states now offer state loans for building construction while fourteen extend loan guarantees for the same purpose. Like IDB revenue bonds, these guarantees reduce the interest charges to individual borrowers.

Direct grants in a sense represent taxation in reverse—with the public purse contributing revenue to private enterprise rather than private enterprise contributing tax dollars toward the provision of public goods and services. Most often, this kind of aid takes the form of a jurisdiction constructing a plant and renting it to the firm for a nominal fee, often $1 a year.

MOST OF these special incentives for business have been enacted since the 1960s, with the 1970s witnessing particularly dramatic growth in the size and rate of state giveaways. By 1978, some states were offering packages including as many as 27 different financial assistance, tax incentive and special service incentives to business that would locate in their state. New York, Connecticut, Minnesota, New Jersey, North Dakota, and Oklahoma led the list, while only seven states offered fewer than ten such subsidies. Businesses do not pass up the opportunity to play these states against each other, and as *Business Week* has noted, "Competition among regions, states, and municipalities for industry and jobs appears to be escalating into fierce—perhaps ruinous— warfare.''

From the states' point of view, of course, the rationale for competing against each other and offering significant financial incentives for business seems clear. Using lower taxes, better financing arrangements and other inducements, a state can present a cost differential—and thus a real economic benefit—to a firm considering a location decision. But in reality the actual cost differential between one state and another (which in most cases is slight in any event) seems to matter less than the *symbolic* use of incentives as a signal to business of a "pro-business attitude" or "good business climate.'' Indeed, for all of the hoopla associated with tax breaks and other giveaways, researchers are in almost unanimous agreement that:

• investment inducements almost never do what they were intended to accomplish;

• even when they appear to entail no direct costs, they are enormously expensive in foregone tax revenue; and

• such subsidies end up being windfall profits for the largest and most powerful corporations.

The evidence pointing to these conclusions is overwhelming. For example, it is clear that local tax rates—or abatements—are not nearly as significant as other factors which the state cannot control, such as wage rates. Since for a typical business labor costs might be 20 times larger than state and local tax payments, a 2 percent wage differential is as important as a 40 percent differential in tax rates. Given the fact that the actual difference in tax rates between Frostbelt and Sunbelt states often amounts to no more than a single percentage point, it is easy to see that a tiny difference in wage rates will be a far more important location consideration.

Not only is there significant statistical evidence discrediting the alleged importance of business subsidies, but industrialists and businessmen, in survey after survey, indicate they themselves do not put much stock in tax differences when it comes to locating or relocating their establishments.

Further, since states find themselves in competition, logic would dictate that they would in any event adopt incentive policies that would follow each other's lead. Noting this tendency in the 1960s, the Advisory Commission on Intergovernmental Relations warned that, "Interstate competition will inevitably dissipate states' efforts to attract industry, and may oblige Congress to curb the practice through federal legislation."

THE STUNNING conclusion, then, is that the use of tax and financial incentives—the centerpiece of state and local efforts to keep capital from moving or to attract new capital—is of practically no use in actually influencing decisions on capital movement. The billions spent each year on business subsidies are spent in vain. As the report of a set of interviews with businesspeople in Connecticut concluded, incentives did not actually produce any business behavior that would not have occurred otherwise. Instead, the incentives functioned as a windfall for the companies at the expense of taxpayers.

This was certainly true of a special tax giveaway which was touted in Massachusetts as creating jobs. A survey carried out at Harvard University in 1974 studied the impact of a $500 job creation tax credit just passed into law (with a great deal of publicity) in that state. The researchers conducted formal interviews with 84 percent of all those who had applied to the state for this subsidy. They found, to the obvious chagrin of the state, that not a single job in these sixteen firms was filled in response to the tax credit. Rather the firm first filled the jobs in normal response to market demands, and then later claimed the credit when their accountants found that they were eligible for the subsidy.

Unhappily, the losses of tax incentives are not limited to the actual financial giveaways, as substantial as they may be. Subsidizing the private sector can also involve an extraordinary paradox: *investment incentives can ultimately destroy more jobs than they create.* Money that is used to subsidize business is money that could have been used by government to provide resources for other purposes—for example, public service positions. Dollars spent on tax subsidies cannot be spent on public schools, police, fire protection, or sanitation.

In issuing Industrial Development Bonds, the federal government creates a multi-billion dollar tax loss which is more than double the annual outlay of AFDC welfare payments for the more than 3 million families on assistance. Presumably the least inflationary response to this loss of federal revenue is to cut spending by an equivalent amount, a policy that in some cases could clearly reduce net employment.

The *Wall Street Journal* recently raised the specter that tax abatement fever may be "out of control," forcing cutbacks in public services and deepening the fiscal crisis. Other stories appearing regularly in major U.S. cities confirm the *Journal's* fear.

In 1977 alone, the Cleveland city council approved abatements estimated to cost as much as $20 million over the next 20 years. In Michigan, existing tax incentives could cost the state $50 million a year and local communities another $30 million by 1986. New York City auditors argue the nearly bankrupt city may have needlessly granted more than $56 million in tax breaks to blue-chip corporations such as IBM, F. W. Woolworth, and several leading hotel chains. St. Louis granted abatements in 1975-1976 on $116 million of new construction which will deprive the school system of some $40 million over the next 25 years. Similar stories are almost regular fare in Detroit, Toledo, Boston, Cincinnati, New York, St. Louis, Hartford, Kansas City, Sacramento, Lansing, Cleveland, and Columbus, to name but a few.

THE CONTINUING erosion of taxes will mean the inadvertent deterioration of essential public services and, it is argued, will not only bring an immediate loss in public sector jobs but may very well be self-defeating in terms of long-term *private sector* job creation, because eventually poor public services even more than "high taxes" will keep firms from investing. The current boom in southern New Hampshire has just such dark overtones.

This story of a public policy gone wrong has one more unintended and unhappy consequence. That is, that the primary beneficiaries of these government windfalls are the largest corporations—not the smaller firms that might, in fact, be forced by market competition to pay attention to tiny cost differentials between locations.

For example, the largest companies are able to dominate the IDB market for several reasons, including their superior credit rating and their ability to exploit geographic diversity to play various bond markets against each other.

The larger firms are also able to package IDBs with tax abatements and therefore obtain a larger proportion of both. Moreover, their size gives them the resources with which to play off one community against another until they receive the largest possible abatement. Smaller

firms, just as they have little clout in the market, often have relatively less clout with City Hall or state development offices than do the Fortune 500.

How can so many communities fall into the trap of offering such costly and self-defeating "incentives"? Clearly one reason is that in their desperation they see no other viable means of protecting jobs from the very real threat of capital flight.

THE OTHER piece of our current structure of public policies dealing with corporate flight is the limited use of public funds as "welfare" payments to compensate for economic dislocation. Unfortunately, these programs were never designed specifically to help the victims of plant closings. In such a program government revenues could be used to provide severance pay, retraining, or migration assistance to the workers (and families) left in the lurch. Instead, some compensation has been available to the unemployed in the form of state-provided unemployment insurance, job retraining programs, and public assistance. Particularly for non-union workers, these three programs often serve as the first, second, and ultimate lines of defense against poverty. Yet while they are used, none of these programs are particularly well suited to the task of compensating those adversely affected by plant shutdowns *per se*.

Unemployment insurance, for example, replaces only a fraction of weekly earnings, and under normal circumstances is only available for a maximum of twenty-six weeks. Given the finding that a significant minority of plant closing victims are without jobs for more than six months, it provides only temporary, and usually inadequate relief.

Trade Readjustment Assistance (TRA) augments unemployment compensation for those workers who can prove that liberalized trade relations "contributed importantly" to the elimination of their jobs. But until late 1977 few workers were designated as eligible for this program.

By 1977, the allocation for the expanded program was still only $230 million, but workers were being deemed eligible at an accelerating rate. Between December 1977 and April 1978, for example, the *Wall Street Journal* reported that close to 30,000 workers were cleared for assistance.

But even the new program goes only so far. Few workers find it worthwhile to take advantage of the training assistance and even fewer the migration allowances. As a result, the program has been criticized because it provides little more than unemployment-type benefits without enabling the worker to obtain future employment.

This criticism of TRA can conceivably be generalized to the whole welfare strategy as such. The benefits at least theoretically available to workers are not inconsequential, but workers tend not to use them (except for the cash assistance), according to a Federal Reserve study. That report blames the problem on the delivery of services and the difficulty of motivating workers to make use of them. If worker assistance is to be successful, the study suggests, "Greater efforts will have to be made to counsel, place, and train affected workers."

This lack of motivation is surely not independent of the fact that comparable jobs for (often middle-aged or older) workers trained in specific skills are hard to find, so that retraining or migration assistance is of little value. Moreover, many workers who have established themselves in their communities have no desire to pull up stakes when their plant closes down. The relocation assistance and the cash benefits may help them to put bread on the table and continue to pay the mortgage, but do nothing to compensate for the grieving often associated with being involuntarily uprooted.

Nevertheless, expanding on the concept behind TRA still seems worthwhile. A need exists, for instance, for extending adjustment assistance to cover workers who are laid off as a result of plant shutdown (or any large-scale permanent layoff) regardless of the cause—imports, a runaway shop, or simple bankruptcy. In this regard, the experience in Western European countries is worth noting. The governments in these countries have tried as much as possible to fully compensate workers who lose their jobs through no fault of their own. Awareness of the social consequences that face American workers who lose their jobs because of capital flight strongly suggests the need for adopting some of these measures here at home.

Even so, as the social costs of corporate flight and the cost of compensation continue to escalate, industrial governments will find that a more practical solution would be to enact laws that would help prevent such problems in the first place.

National
Distributor
LYON METAL PRO UCTS
RAIL ROAD
CROSSING
5
TRACKS
STOP
ON RED
SIGNAL

Chapter Five
WHERE WE CAN GO FROM HERE

JUST AS conglomerates and multinational corporations are here to stay, so are the economic and political forces which encourage the rapid, worldwide movement of capital. And just as the 1980s bring new demands on that capital—especially here in America, where "reindustrialization" has become part of our everyday vocabulary—the need to allocate resources wisely becomes increasingly critical.

Certainly the ability to disinvest quickly and transfer assets without encumbrance is valuable to any business, and indeed such corporate behavior has contributed heavily to many profitable balance sheets and hefty returns on investment.

But there is another, more important balance sheet: the calculation of the net effect on society—what has been called the *public* balance sheet. It is there, when we look beyond the profit picture of any one corporation or industry, that we see that an investment decision beneficial to one company may well have a substantial negative impact on society as a whole. The immediate social violence which a plant closing might cause for hundreds of families has a multiplied effect on communities and even regions, but rarely is there any calculation of this extraordinary public cost.

Proponents of unregulated capital movement argue that it helps the economy work efficiently. But it is not hard to see that it often has precisely the opposite effect. Spending the tens or even hundreds of millions of dollars it might take to rebuild shattered communities, in return for slightly better profits for a runaway company, does not seem to be a very good deal from the point of view of the average taxpayer. This is especially so if those slightly better profits yield no net increase in national output.

Of course, there is no public balance sheet to look

over down at City Hall. There is no mechanism for putting a brake on the velocity of shifting investment if the social cost is too great. As we have seen, what we have instead are community tax giveaways that ultimately benefit only corporations, and a few welfare-type programs, after the fact, that apply a small bandage to the open wound.

What is needed is a course of action that in the short term will prevent some shutdowns and lessen the impacts of others, and that in the long term will lead to rational, democratic planning of important economic decisions. At a minimum, monitoring and directing the flow of private capital (a strategy used often in Western Europe and Japan) will enhance community stabilization and worker security. Even more useful might be significant encouragement of worker or community-owned and managed ventures, and even selective nationalization within key industries. It is important to note that this kind of comprehensive planning will help the economy as a whole function as efficiently and as productively as possible.

THERE ARE a number of useful changes that can be made right away. For workers who are members of unions, collective bargaining represents the first line of defense against precipitous dislocation from plant closings. The last few years have witnessed several successful negotiations to protect jobs and wages or at least to guarantee severance benefits.

The major electrical unions, for example, have won an agreement from the Westinghouse Corporation for two years' prior notice in the event of a partial or complete shutdown. The agreement also covers layoffs connected with changes in product lines, and gives the unions limited access to the company's records pertaining to longterm investment and production plans. Other new contracts between the United Food and Commercial Workers (UFCW) and several meat-packing firms prohibit the firms from closing a plant and then reopening it on a non-union basis within five years. And a contract between the Amalgamated Clothing and Textile Workers Union (ACTWU) and one garment firm includes the provision that during the term of the agreement the employer will not remove his plants from the cities in which they are located without the consent of the union.

But these victories do not mean that the labor movement has solved the problem. Not at all. Not only does three-quarters of the American labor force have no direct trade union protection whatsoever, but those whose jobs *are* covered by collective bargaining agreements receive really very little protection from plant closings or large cutbacks. Most advance notification agreements call for one week's notice or less, and fully half of all American workers covered in some respect by a contract receive no income protection of any kind.

Another problem for unions is the lack of maneuvering room they see under current labor law. Frequently they feel constrained by the bargaining mandates of "wages, hours, and working conditions" and thus do not bring job protection to the table at all. A union agenda for labor law reform also includes repeal of Section 14(b) of the Taft-Hartley Act, which encourages the open shop and the consequent suppression of workers' rights and living standards, as well as clarification of the problem of successorship, with the goal of making it an unfair labor practice for an employer who assumes ownership or operation of an ongoing business to refuse to assume all of the terms and conditions of a predecessor contract.

The need for labor law reform, or the relatively small number of unionized workers, are not by themselves the only problems with a collective bargaining approach to dislocation. Bargaining is also generally incapable of providing for the rebuilding of the local economic base in the wake of major shutdowns. A better way to address all of the problems of corporate flight simultaneously, and provide a comprehensive response, is through the enactment of new plant closing legislation. In this area the European experience provides a useful lesson. One study by American trade unionists noted, for example, that Sweden, West Germany and England all had legislative programs for coping with the adverse effects of economic dislocation. In all three countries, corporations are required to give substantial advance notice of closings or layoffs, and in the latter case negotiation often results in layoffs only by attrition. And all three countries have programs for retraining and reemployment of dislocated workers at the company's or the government's expense. The same study, while recognizing that such programs would doubtless be opposed by American companies as costly and burdensome, noted that many of those very same companies have been operating profitably in these three foreign countries for several decades.

AMERICAN efforts to pass plant closing legislation began in 1974, when then-Senator Walter Mondale (D-Minn.) and Congressman William Ford (D-Mich.) introduced into Congress the National Employment Priorities Act (NEPA). This would have created a board to investigate employee complaints, to rule on the necessity of plant shutdowns, and to recommend that the government withhold tax benefits if the shutdowns were determined to be unjustified.

NEPA had a major flaw, however: it lacked criteria for judging when a plant closing was justified, and thus gave companies generous government subsidies for not relocating if they so much as announced that they were considering the idea. In any case, the bill was never even reported out of committee.

After NEPA's failure, the effort to organize plant closing legislation shifted to the states. In 1975, the Ohio Public Interest Campaign (OPIC) was put together by labor unions, senior citizens, civil rights and consumer groups, and church groups to organize resistance to the wave of Midwest plant closings; by 1977 OPIC had drafted the Community Readjustment Act, which was introduced in the state legislature. It also did not succeed, but was redrafted and is now winning wide support. Its six key provisions have come to define the basic agenda for legislation (now being considered in at least eleven other states):

1. Prior notification of major cutbacks and total shutdowns.

2. Discharge or severance payments for all workers, whether or not they are unionized.

3. Continuation of health insurance coverage for some period following the layoffs, paid by the company.

4. Increased rights of transfer to other plants or stores in the company's system.

5. Lump sum payment to local governments, to help finance economic redevelopment.

6. Preparation by joint company-union-government committees of economic impact statements, to facilitate redevelopment efforts.

An even more comprehensive agenda, relating to the same points, has been put forward by the unions participating in the European study. Plant closing legislation has been introduced or is pending in close to 20 states, and is being supported by many other citizen groups, including the Coalition to Save Jobs (Massachusetts), the Pennsylvania Public Interest Campaign, the Illinois Public Action Council, the Indiana Citizen Action Coalition, the Community Labor Organizing Committee (Rhode Island), the New York Citizens Alliance, and Oregon Fair Share.

On the federal level, a new version of the National Employment Priorities Act was introduced in 1979. This NEPA, known as the "Ford-Riegle" bill, mandates prenotification, severance pay, successorship, transfer rights, protection of benefits for a period following shutdown, grants and loans to some ailing businesses, economic redevelopment assistance to local governments, and assistance to workers who want to buy businesses which are closing in order to run them as cooperatives. Several other bills also support the idea of worker ownership, including one which would require the Small Business Administration to extend its entire range of technical and financial services to small worker-owned companies and cooperatives.

A KEY short-term element of all of the proposed plant closing legislation is the requirement that a firm's management provide advance notification of a planned shutdown or a major cutback. Without prenotification, not only are unemployment services severely taxed by unexpected demand, but efforts to develop the facility for other uses, or even to rescue existing operations by some means, are often precluded.

If, on the other hand, a shutdown notice is issued well in advance, then workers, unions, local governments and planners have an opportunity to consider alternative responses and act before people are actually thrown out of work. At the same time, to facilitate the

process the company contemplating the shutdown should provide important financial and employment information—for which many of the categories have already been identified in a report from the Federal Trade Commission. Unfortunately, workers often lack access to proprietary financial information, and thus have some difficulty determining whether a community or worker buyout could succeed.

There are other ways to provide an early-warning system for plant closings besides prenotification. One is to develop statistical models which can predict the probability that a particular firm may be contemplating a move or be in financial difficulty and considering restructuring or bankruptcy. At least two such models already exist, and have successfully predicted changes up to two years in advance. However, once again complete financial information—often not available—is needed from companies themselves. Another problem is that predictive models are generally useful for entire firms, not for any one plant, and thus would not be able to predict an individual shift in operations or a closing.

The best system for providing early warning may well come from workers themselves, and several unions are already training "reconnaissance personnel" in the plant or office to watch for signs that management is contemplating or implementing major disinvestment. Failure to maintain or replace old equipment, plans for impending automation, severe and continued cost-cutting, efforts to sell off real estate holdings, and the opening of other branch operations performing the same tasks elsewhere are all possible signs that a shutdown may be around the corner.

Besides finding ways to anticipate a shutdown and prepare workers and the community for its effects, there are other more positive steps to take. A community and its workers can best protect themselves against dislocation caused by large-scale private disinvestment by cultivating the ability to redevelop the local economy. Such rebuilding can start by a careful examination of the feasibility (and desirability) of a worker or community buy-out of the establishment which is being closed. There may also be room in such a program for local, decentralized management of nationalized firms in key sectors of the economy. In either case, new development finance mechanisms would have to be created to get the right kinds of capital into the hands of the builders who need it most.

To take the first case, the movement for worker ownership has been especially active in recent years. Between 1974 and 1979, some seventy large private businesses in the U.S. were bought either by their employees or by various community organizations; about 70 percent of these purchases came after closings related to corporate or conglomerate divestiture. Overall, by 1979, more than 1,000 employee stock ownership plans (ESOP's) were in operation in different companies, with workers owning the majority interest in perhaps 100 of these. Productivity, wages, and reported employee job satisfaction were all typically higher in such workplaces, and profitability was actually greater, the greater the share of the equity owned by the employees.

Unfortunately, worker ownership also presents some problems, and each individual case has to be carefully studied and planned before its implementation. For example, the workers who purchased the GAF Corporation's asbestos mining operation in Vermont learned that when individuals own unequal amounts of stock, market forces can make it virtually impossible for them to resist selling out to entrepreneurs who show up with large cash offers after the business has been successfully turned around. The obvious remedy is to distribute stock on a one-share-per-worker basis, if not explicitly assigning all shares to the collective itself.

Other potential problems with worker buy-outs include the unpleasant fact that conventional businesses may try to undermine those ventures which are successful, and that often the market for the product of the reopened plant is still controlled by the old company—probably now doing business somewhere else, with cheaper labor. The use of employee pension funds to finance buy-outs is also a risky game, in which workers are betting their pensions to save their jobs.

The long-range strategy of developing a progressive program for redeveloping local economies affected by business closings and cutbacks converges with another important issue: the direct public investment in, and ownership of, at least a few major companies in such key sectors of the economy as housing, transportation, energy, communications, and basic materials. The case for such "benchmark" public enterprise is based on the need to gain direct access to information about the true costs of production in a sector, to be in a position to replace outputs or services if they are withheld by private corporations, to offer genuine price competition in the face of inflationary private mark-ups, and to have an instrument for directly creating at least some jobs in places where they are most needed. Abandonment of a plant by private business creates an opportunity to introduce carefully targeted public enterprise, eliminating (or at least reducing) the necessity for outright nationalization.

However, a poorly planned program of public enterprise development can amount to little more than a bailout for management and the saddling of workers or government with an unprofitable "lemon" if careful research and monitoring are not done by the community itself.

AS SHOULD be expected, business interests are actively opposing these changes across the board, from government participation in public enterprise development, to efforts at worker ownership, to prenotification, and to legislation. And every indicator points to that opposition getting stronger during the 1980s, particularly with a Republican in the White House. Recently dozens of books, articles, and speeches have denounced the efforts of labor and community groups to—as business spokespeople put it—hold industry for "ransom." And the political and economic pressure being applied to legislators and public officials, at the federal, state and local levels, shows no signs of abating.

Management's primary offensive weapon is the threat to stop expanding operations—or fail to locate in the first place—in states which pass legislation regulating the mobility of private capital. The same tactics are used, of course, to bludgeon states and communities into tax giveaways and business subsidies.

And the tactics work. Public officials shrink in fear from the possibility of being labeled as friendly to labor—the common phrase is "having an unfriendly business climate"—or from consideration of restrictive plant closing legislation. As the head of a corporate lobbying group put it when testifying against such legislation in Massachusetts: "Even serious consideration of this bill would be raising a sign on the borders of this state that investment isn't welcome here."

Advance notification of cutbacks or shutdowns is the element in proposed legislation which consistently draws the heaviest fire. Opponents argue both that such prenotification is impractical—presumably because such decisions are often made quite abruptly—and that the announcement of an intended closing might cause a drop in productivity and a loss of skilled and semiskilled workers.

Both propositions are contradicted by evidence. Many case studies of plant closings (not to mention the observations of workers themselves) show that many shutdowns were contemplated and decisions made years in advance. Further, multinational U.S. companies operating in Europe not only have been able to provide the prenotification required by their labor contracts but have done so with no readily apparent drop in productivity. (It is worth noting that almost all European firms have had to accept prenotification—in England and Germany since the 1960s). It may well be that, rather than leaving suddenly because of the announcement of a future shutdown, workers are more likely to leave because of the uncertainty surrounding a *possible* plant closing. Prenotification enables workers to plan, instead of acting out of misinformed anticipation.

In fact, there are only two cases of corporate investment behavior where plant closing legislation would impose a high short-term cost on the owner: the conglomerate acquisition of a local business which is operated as a "cash cow" and then shut down, or a low-wage "fly-by-night" sweatshop. And both of these types of investment are in many ways detrimental to the economic health and stability of a community. For a company with a healthy long-term investment strategy, legislation should in no way threaten their ability to make profits.

NEVERTHELESS, BUSINESS has dug in and is ready to fight any and all legislative efforts —indeed, any forms of restriction on capital mobility. The facts of the matter can be put quite bluntly, as in this quote from an aide to the Governor of Rhode Island, a state which at the time was considering a plant closing bill: "Industry doesn't like government telling them what they can do and what they can't do."

And business is in a strong position to pursue its interests: the new economic power of conglomerates, the easy availability of cheap overseas sources of labor, high unemployment and slow growth in the U.S., and now a business-oriented President combine to put labor at a disadvantage in the difficult fight against uncontrolled corporate disinvestment and flight.

In this new class war of the 1980s between labor and management, labor has no choice but to aggressively organize, within and even more importantly across regional and national borders. Labor must participate in drawing up a public balance sheet, and in establishing a national mandate for rational, coordinated economic planning—providing both for growth and revitalization and for equity and community stability. In a clear new agenda for progressives the case must be made for controlling the velocity of capital in order to account for its social costs. If that case is not made, if the battle over totally unregulated corporate flight is not joined, then the war will be over—with disastrous consequences for workers everywhere—in the North, in the South, in private enterprise and in the public sector. No worker is immune.

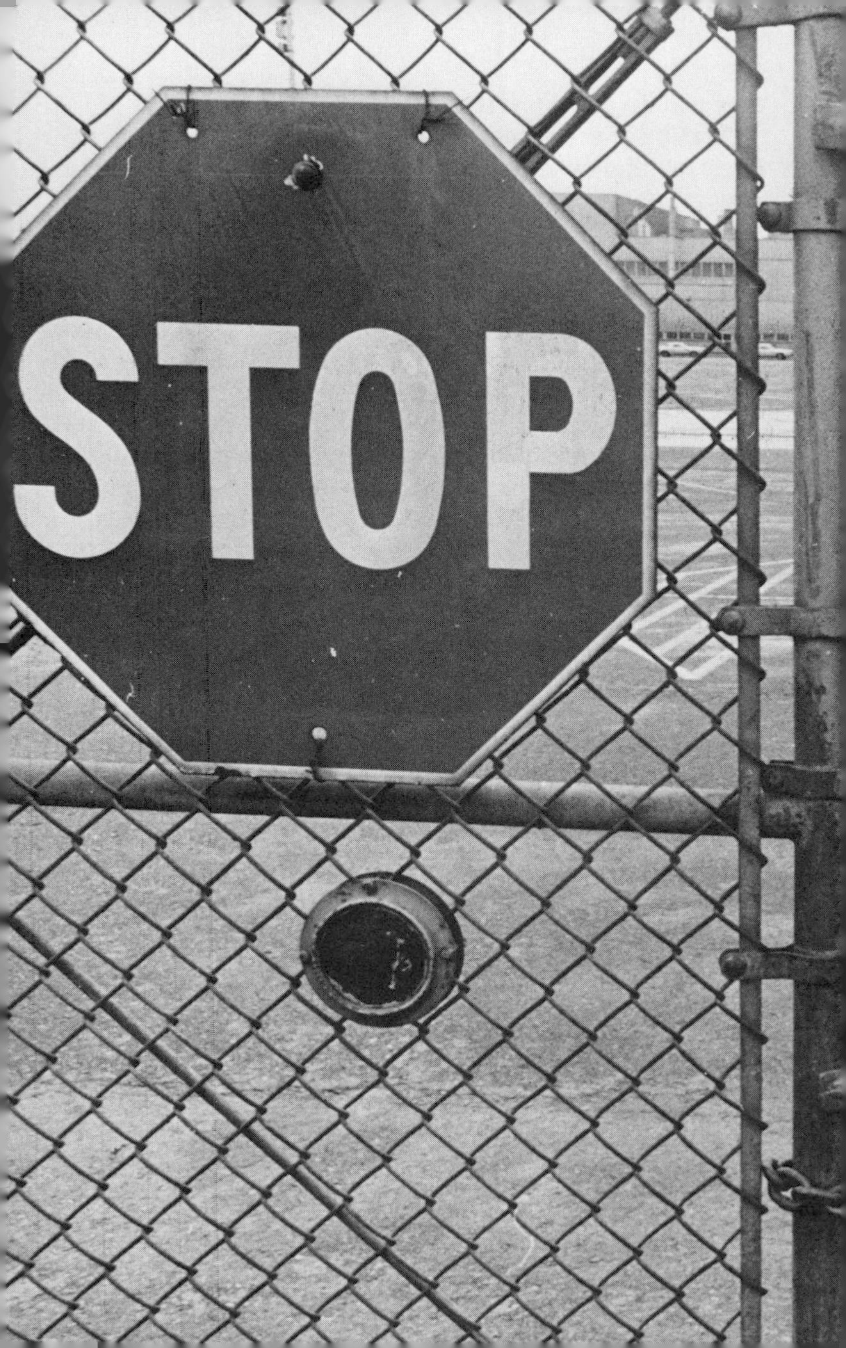
STOP